The Beverage Coaster: A Book of Life Thoughts

101 QUOTES AND THOUGHTS TO HELP
YOU THROUGH THE ROCKY ROAD
OF LIFE (OR A BOOK TO REST YOUR
FAVORITE BEVERAGE ON!)

Jay Carlson

authorHOUSE®

AuthorHouse™
1663 Liberty Drive
Bloomington, IN 47403
www.authorhouse.com
Phone: 1-800-839-8640

First published by AuthorHouse 10/18/2010

ISBN: 978-1-4520-8676-7 (sc)
ISBN: 978-1-4520-8675-0 (e)

Library of Congress Control Number: 2010914904

Printed in the United States of America

This book is printed on acid-free paper.

Foreward

This compilation of WISDOM'S PEARLS is dedicated to you. Jay has captured life's rich nuggets and placed them into a bottle, like sand in an hourglass. Each thought, fundamental, yet profound, will help you carve a path as you journey toward your destiny. I trust that as you read them, you will read with, not only your eyes, but your heart, your spirit and embrace an "Aha" moment...EVERY DAY!

Valerie G. Foye

"Tuesdays are good
because they remind
you that Monday is
long over & is a long
time coming again."

"Sometimes a good
friend is hard to find,
but it's even harder to
lose them."

"Sometimes the unexpected just happens"

⚜

"Life is full of ups and downs as well as surprises. It's those surprises that help us deal with life."

"It's what we feel that makes us who we are. It's what we don't feel that makes us who we aren't."

"Take a moment to breathe in the air and take a breath of life"

"Kids can make you happy, kids can make you crazy. It's the happiness they bring though that makes you so crazy about them."

※

"Sometimes I need a compass to tell me which direction I'm being driven crazy."

"The world is like a giant book filled with an infinite number of interesting characters."

"It takes an individual to ask the question but it takes a community or group to solve the problem."

"If you're strong, positive and happy, it's contagious & will carry over to others."

"A momentary lapse of reason can have permanent consequences"

"Life experiences can help move us forward. It's the lack of those experiences that hold us back."

"Music comes from the heart. Music comes from the soul. Music comes from anywhere you want it to and can take you to wherever you want to go."

"When you think of
it, if we constantly
underestimate
ourselves, the outcomes
in life can only be
successful ones."

"Beautiful nights
can lead to the most
incredible mornings"

"Be who you are and shine. Be who you aren't and no one will ever see your glow."

"Having fun is part of living. Living is part of having fun."

"Smiling is a way of saying, good morning world, I'm part of you and happy for it."

"Take a trip somewhere, anywhere, even if it's to a special place in your imagination."

"Don't let your dreams stay just dreams. Make them come true."

"Love doesn't come easy but it's easy to hold on to if you work hard at it."

"Money isn't the root of all evil, but you can sure grow some nice things with it."

"Having many friends is a luxury. Having one good true friend is priceless."

"Do what you do best
and do your absolute
best at it"

"Reinventing yourself
as you age is an exciting
part of life"

"If you love and respect
the person you are,
others will too"

"If you keep finding
yourself saying that
'Life gets in the way'
for things you meant
to do but haven't done,
just step to the side
every now and then."

"Yesterday is in the books and tomorrow is always another day. But for now, focus on today."

"Never let go of your childhood. It's what grounds us, it's what makes us who we are as adults and most importantly, it keeps us who we are as individuals."

"Loving someone can be a beautiful thing. Liking that person as well can be oh so rewarding."

"Each of us has our own path to follow. We may stray from that path from time to time, but hopefully find our way back to it eventually."

"Shine like the sun.
Beam like the moon.
Be bright like the stars.
Illuminate yourself and
those around you."

"Sometimes your
conscience can be your
best friend"

"Listen to your heart,
but only when your
ears are wide open."

⚜

"Be gracious and take
what you are given, but
do great things with
it."

"Idle minds can make
for a slow and boring
day"

"Plant some thoughts
and harvest your
dreams"

"Sometimes closed-mindedness can overshadow an open heart"

⚜

"Never forget those who have helped you get where you are because without them, you might not have gotten as far."

"Live the fabulous life you've been given. No one else is gonna do it for you."

"If you pass a stranger on the street, give them a smile. You might not get one back but it'll still make you feel good inside."

"Having complete days
to yourself is great, but
then again, who would
you complain to?"

⚜

"Each of us is here
to make some kind
of difference in this
world. No matter
how big or how small,
each contribution is
different and special in
its own way."

"Time doesn't slow down, but you can, to make every moment last longer."

"Everyone has their moments of failure at one point or another, but those are not nearly as memorable as our moments of success, no matter how small they may be."

"Having someone
on your back all the
time is a heavy load to
carry, but somehow we
always seem to make
it through and lighten
that load."

"If people tell you
that you got up on the
wrong side of the bed,
start sleeping on the
other side."

"Having a family
to love is a life long
privilege. Don't ruin
it by neglecting them.
Remember, not
everyone can be so
lucky."

"You'd be surprised
how much weight your
shoulders can carry if
you maintain a positive
attitude."

"We may age externally but you can stay internally young, eternally, if you really try."

❧❁☙

"Honesty is like a double-edged sword. It can make people feel good and it can hurt people sometimes as well. But in the end, it is always the right thing and you will be respected for it."

"When you feel like you have too much on your 'plate', it's time to grab a 'platter'."

"Sometimes a good rain can cleanse away all of the B.S. you've had to put up with all day or all week."

"Keep your family
close as well as your
friends, because when
all is said and done,
friends are family."

"Watching your
kids grow can be so
fulfilling, but do they
have to grow up so
fast? If only time would
move at our chosen
pace."

"Don't be a couch potato all the time. Get up and move, at least to a chair."

※

"As you age, your parents take care of you. As your kids age, you take care of them. As your parents age, you take care of them and as you age, your kids take care of you. It's a beautiful and complete cycle of life."

"Be real. Be you. Be the 'real you'."

"It's wonderful having a dog. First they pee on your carpet, then they tear a hole in your sock, and before you know it, words are coming out of your mouth that you've only heard in R-rated movies. But even with all that, in the end, it's still a wonderful experience."

"Every answer has a question. It's coming up with the right question that is often the hard part."

"Swallow your pride when you need to. Just be careful not to choke on it."

"Reach out to an old friend every now and then. You might be surprised how much has changed with them and in turn within you."

"No matter how many times you get knocked down in life, keep getting up off the mat, you can make it to the final round."

"It's great having a wife. Someone who's constantly there for you. Someone who will always care for you. Someone you can call your best friend. Someone who makes your house a 'home'."

"Be comfortable in your own shoes. If you're not, try another size."

"Listening to an old song that you haven't heard in years is great, isn't it? It brings back this wave of past experiences and memories that sort of rush all over you, all while staying in the present."

"Sometimes getting a simple pat on the back for a job well done can be invaluable."

"Be a good sport and poke fun at yourself every now and then. It'll probably make you laugh and that makes it all worth it."

"Dating is a lot like buying clothes or shoes. You just keep trying on different ones and different styles until you find the one that fits just right."

"Putting up a brave
front is good but
staying brave inside is
even better."

"You may have many
disappointments or
failures in life, however
perseverance can be
your greatest success
story."

"If you occasionally think that life isn't going your way, just turn around and change directions from time to time."

"I'd rather spend a cold day with a 'warm' person than a warm day with a 'cold' person."

"Don't fall short on your beliefs. Stand tall for what you believe in."

***

"Forget about the glass as always being half empty or half full. Try looking at it as always being completely full and see what happens."

"Staying happy and positive is a lifelong project. Stay involved in your project."

"Don't go and get tangled up in someone else's line, pick another place to fish. You might just catch something good."

"An ordinary
person can make an
extraordinary life for
themselves."

"Having the freedom
to do what you want
is a wonderful thing,
however wasting that
freedom on things you
don't need is not so
wonderful."

"Life is like a never-ending puzzle, not really meant to be 'figured' out."

"Instead of holding grudges, hold the ones you love. It's much more satisfying."

"An old piece of furniture can easily be discarded, but the right person can refinish it and make it like new again. Sometimes we just need to 'refinish' ourselves to make life new again."

"It's great to branch out and try new things but every now and then it's okay to re-try old things as well."

"It's wonderful having an understanding spouse to who loves you as well as a loving one who understands you."

"A broken bone can heal easily, but a broken heart or spirit, not so much. Be mindful of every step you take."

"Give yourself a chance to excel in something foreign to you. In time, you might just find yourself a natural."

"Even if you and your partner have been together for quite a while, take time to rediscover each other every now and then. You may be amazed and surprised at what you'll learn."

"Many of life's best moments are the small ones that don't seem special at the time, but when you look back upon them years later, take on a sort of 'greatness' that you can't put a price tag on."

"With every season change, endless opportunities open up for you to explore."

"Sometimes you follow your head and sometimes you follow your heart. Isn't it great though when they both tell you the same thing?"

"We are all mathematicians in a sense. That is, we all have the capability of turning a negative into a positive."

"Unlock yourself and let the world see the positive and confident side of you, instead of keeping it hidden inside."

"There's so much going on around us every day that we may take for granted. Take a moment to not just hear, but to 'listen' to all the interesting sounds of life."

"Some people may know where they're going but have forgotten where they've been."

❧⁂❧

"The 'career path' is a long one with many lanes and twists and turns. Be whatever you want to be and remember it's okay to change lanes if you want."

"If you think about
it, our kids are our
greatest assets. They
have a wealth of
memories to share,
bring us all the
happiness in the world
which is priceless,
and then carry on
the family name and
replenish those funds."

"A dream come true is
born from a great idea"

"If you're a fan of the 'arts', rediscover the art of communication, it's a wonderful medium."

"Peace and love are not outdated concepts… they carry over from generation to generation."

"Grab your favorite beverage and drink a toast to life"